Henry Pellatt

Fitzhenry & Whiteside Limited

Contents

Flint, David, 1938-
Henry Pellatt

(The Canadians)

Bibliography: p. 64
ISBN 0-88902-659-9

1. Pellatt, Henry Mill, Sir, 1859-1939. 2. Capitalists and financiers—Ontario — Toronto—Biography. I. Series.

FC3097.41.P44F55 971.3'541'00924 C78-001405-7
F1059.5.T6853P44

The Author

David Flint has written biographies of William Lyon Mackenzie and John Strachan and a study of the Hutterites. He is head of the history department at A.Y. Jackson Secondary School in North York.

The Canadians A continuing series

General Editor: Robert Read
Consulting Editor: Roderick Stewart
Designer: Jack Steiner

Printed and bound in Canada

Prologue

Sir Henry Mill Pellatt was the builder of Casa Loma—a tangible and permanent reflection of the character of this massive man. He will be remembered as long as this monument stands.

One historian has called Pellatt "perhaps the most romantic and most spectacular citizen whom Toronto has ever known." Some of his contemporaries considered him the "Cecil Rhodes of Canada" and "the most generous and enthusiastic soldier" in the country. He built the high reputation of the Queen's Own Rifles regiment and basked in the glory it brought him.

As a young man, Henry made his reputation as a financial wizard. Personally reticent but flamboyant with his wealth, he was best known in his time as "Pellatt the plunger", an unrestrained investor and manipulator of his

Henry Pellatt's monumental home, Casa Loma

own and other people's fortunes. Although at his death in 1939 Pellatt left only $35 000, in his prime he was said to be worth $17 million and enjoying it immensely.

Pellatt's importance as a Canadian was not, however, in his daring financial career, but in his attempts to develop this country's natural resources and utilities under private ownership, without foreign investment or government grants.

The Pellatt Tradition Chapter 1

Henry Mill Pellatt was born in Kingston, Ontario on January 6, 1859. He was the eldest son of six children born to Henry Pellatt, a British immigrant who had come to Canada in 1852, and Emma Holland, a Peterborough native. Although Kingston, the capital of pre-Confederation Canada, seemed to offer good business potential, the family moved within two years of Henry's birth to Toronto, a growing industrial and commercial community. Henry Sr. was employed in the Bank of British North America. Within four decades, his son Henry would become one of Toronto's best-known residents.

As a growing boy, Pellatt was part of a well-educated family confident of its place in British history. Genealogists have traced the Pellatts through church records to Sussex, where they could have settled before the Norman Conquest in 1066. Down through the centuries, the family has prominently displayed a coat of arms enscribed with *Devant si je puis*—"Foremost if I can"—a motto that young Henry Pellatt took to heart.

During Henry's boyhood, the boundaries of Toronto extended from Lake Ontario north to Bloor Street and from the present-day Canadian National Exhibition grounds in the west to the Don River in the east. It was a predominantly British city. Out of a total population of 44 821 in the census of 1860-1861, 12 441 people were of Irish origin, 7112 English and Welsh, 2961 Scottish and 18 767 of non-French, Canadian origin. There were 2031 Americans, 510 black people and 435 of French descent. The four most common occupations were servants (2872), labourers (2184), clerks (1413) and carpenters (1100). The police force employed a chief constable, three sergeant-majors, six sergeants and 25 constables. The Consumers' Gas Company was already in business, and the Toronto Street Railway had provided horse-drawn public transportation for five years.

The city was the manufacturing centre of Upper

Canada. The Toronto Rolling Mills, a producer of nails, employed 300 people. Three foundries—the St. Lawrence, the Phoenix and Armstrong's—manufactured everything from nuts and bolts to stoves. The Toronto Car Wheel Works made wheels for railway cars. The Gooderham and Worts Distillery had 160 employees who produced 7500 gallons of whisky a year, and the city boasted four breweries, including O'Keefe's. There were many smaller businesses: Neil Currie's Boiler and Still Establishment, a woodworks, cabinet factory, pork-packing plant, safe manufacturer, glue company, spice factory, soap and candle factory, four tobacco manufacturers and the Toronto Knitting and Yarn factory—all serving a population that had doubled in the last 20 years.

As a commercial centre, Toronto was served by the Produce Merchants Exchange, the Board of Trade and the Toronto Exchange—businessmen's organizations devoted to maintaining high levels of commodity exports. Toronto was the shipping base for wheat and barley grown throughout southern Ontario and for flour milled locally. Under the Reciprocity Treaty with the United States from 1854 to 1865, these products had been freely exported south of the border, and money had poured into Toronto in return.

This was the Toronto that had drawn Henry Pellatt Sr. In 1866, he was still employed by the Bank of British North America, the only bank at that time owned and controlled by non-Canadians. (In 1918 it was purchased by the Bank of Montreal.) Its English owners normally recruited help in Britain, a practice that brought new ideas, talent and initiative into Canadian banking. After five years with the Toronto bank, however, Henry Sr. felt that, at age 36, he was ripe for a change in careers.

During 1866, he left the bank and opened his own stockbroking business, reportedly the first of its kind in the city. Previously, brokers had maintained a more general share-trading business, dabbling in commodities such as land, money, flour and produce as well as in stocks and bonds. Pellatt thought that a specialized stock brokerage could succeed, for as Toronto's population and economy grew, enough new companies were being formed and old companies expanded that there were plenty of shares to be traded. Hopefully, sufficient new investors could be found so that his company could make a profit on commissions from stock and bond transactions alone.

The Bank of British North America in Toronto, where Henry Pellatt's father worked after moving from Kingston, Ontario. Banks are important institutions in Canadian economic life, but between 1868 and 1923, nine Canadian banks declared bankruptcy. Why do Canadian banks no longer close because of bankruptcy?

As a partner, Pellatt Sr. took in 21-year-old Edmund B. Osler (1854-1924)—younger brother of William, who became one of the world's most eminent physicians, and Featherstone, who became a judge of the Supreme Court of Canada. Edmund himself later became a bank president and a distinguished Member of Parliament. He was knighted, and his estate in the Rosedale section of Toronto was eventually donated to the city as a park. Osler had begun his career in the Bank of Upper Canada, a pillar of provincial institutional life. The board of directors was a *Who's Who* of Toronto's upper-crust society and included the Honourable George W. Allan, who already had been mayor of Toronto and later became Speaker of the Senate and chancellor of Trinity University. At one time or another he was also the president of almost every cultural organization in the city.

Despite such respected leadership, the Bank of Upper Canada went bankrupt in 1866. In the prosperous decade of the 1850s, the bank had freely loaned money to municipalities, railways and, on mortgages, to property owners with little collateral. This freewheeling lending policy left the bank with insufficient cash reserves in case some calamity occurred and a large amount of money was needed quickly. Dangerous as it may seem, this was common banking practice until the 1920s. The Bank of Upper Canada's financial difficulties began in the early 1860s

While visiting Geneva, Switzerland as a youth, Henry Pellatt posed for this studio portrait.

when it lost both the government and the Grand Trunk Railway accounts to the Bank of Montreal. To make matters worse, the economic depression that followed the end of the American Civil War in 1865 frightened depositors and investors. Towards the end of the summer of 1866, rumours spread that the bank was in financial trouble. An uneasy public began to withdraw deposits, slowly at first but soon in a deluge. There was a run on the bank. By 11:00 a.m., September 18, the Bank of Upper Canada had to close its doors, for there was no more money to reimburse depositors. One of the most prominent Canadian financial institutions was forced into bankruptcy.

The failure of the bank and the gloomy forecasts for business after the Reciprocity Treaty ended did not deter Pellatt and Osler. They joined ranks and gambled that the depression would be short-lived. Both were talented, determined and ambitious businessmen, and their success was the base from which young Henry Pellatt built his own good fortune. Because of his wise business practices, Henry Pellatt Sr., unlike most mid nineteenth-century newcomers, had enough money to send his son to the Toronto Model School and Upper Canada College. Established in 1829, this elite educational institution attempted to teach principles of integrity, responsibility and public service through athletic and academic excellence.

Henry's classroom prowess has not been recorded, but he certainly distinguished himself as an athlete. In 1875 and 1876, he was his schools' running champion. In 1878, after he had left school, Henry won the Dominion mile championship at Montreal in a time of 4:42. A year later in New York, he beat the former United States amateur one-mile champion by less than a stride in a near record time of 4:32. He ran the last 100 yards in an amazing 12 seconds. (This distance was not run under 10 seconds until Jesse Owen's historic 9.8 dash in the 1930s.) The competitive 20-year-old Pellatt was also a prominent Toronto lacrosse player.

As Henry matured, he left teams and track meets behind but continued to use his athlete's ability to anticipate moves and make quick decisions in his business dealings and hobbies. His fierce desire to come in first soon propelled Henry to great daring in the financial world. His competitive nature and keen business sense brought him wealth and prestige, which he greatly enjoyed and spontaneously shared with others.

Chapter 2 Rifles and Lights

The Queen's Own Rifles was the second regiment organized in Canada and during the American Civil War was expanded from six to ten companies. Men of the Queen's Own Rifles wear dark green uniforms to make them poor targets in battle.

Young Henry's life-long interest in the military began in 1866 when he was seven. On the first weekend in June, Irish-American soldiers, called Fenians, invaded Canada near Port Colborne on Lake Erie to try to provoke a war between Great Britain and the United States. The Queen's Own Rifles, plus some other volunteers, were rushed to the frontier to help British regulars fight off the invaders. This was the battle of Ridgeway, and Toronto waited tensely for news from the front.

At this time the Queen's Own became affiliated with Upper Canada College. The school's cadet corps formed the regiment's eleventh company and was called the Upper Canada College Rifle Company. From it were recruited young upper-class men to serve in the Queen's Own Rifles. While the men of the regiment fought at Ridgeway, the boys of Upper Canada College went on sentry duty throughout the city, a rare honour for cadets.

On Sunday, the Toronto churches were filled. Between bulletins read aloud by couriers, citizens bowed their heads in prayers for their sons' lives. By late afternoon the Canadians could claim a victory of sorts, for the Fenians returned to the United States having neither won nor lost the battle.

How did fear of the Fenians influence the decision to link together the colonies of British North America in 1867, thus forming the Dominion of Canada?

At 10:00 that night, an immense crowd greeted the *City of Toronto*, a Port Dalhousie steamer that had crossed Lake Ontario carrying the dead and wounded. Seven members of the Queen's Own Rifles died that day; two of the 21 wounded died later. Most of the city turned out a few days later to pay their respects as a funeral procession stretching almost a kilometre in length took five of the dead to their graves in St. James cemetery. This event had a lasting impact on young Henry Pellatt, and when he turned 18 he joined the Queen's Own Rifles. Almost immediately, Henry was involved in the full regiment's only official action between the battle of Ridgeway and the beginning of World War I. (*Units* of the Queen's Own Rifles served in the North West Rebellion in 1885 and in the South African War of 1900.) But the "battle" was an inglorious one.

Canada was almost entirely dependent upon foreign markets for grain, lumber and other natural resource products. During the world depression of 1875-1880, export sales declined and the overexpanded Ontario railway system was forced to cut back its schedules. Ontario's largest railway, the Grand Trunk, tried to solve its financial difficulties by reducing wages. Late in 1876, its engineers went on strike, a right gained by federal legislation passed four years previously. The railway management defiantly tried to keep the trains running.

In Belleville, the engineers responded by staging a sit-in. Described as "a mob of lawless ruffians and their sympathizers" by the anti-labour Toronto *Globe*, they took over the railway station to prevent passengers and freight from being moved. The mayor of Belleville, at the request of the railway, called out the local militia, but the combination of bitterly cold weather and Christmas season festivities made this unpopular. The few Belleville militiamen who answered the call found the strikers behaving

Funeral service for Canadian volunteers killed in action against the Fenians, June 1866. How is the Canadian militia organized today and what are its duties?

peacefully and so refused to "attack" the railway station. On New Year's Day 1877, the frustrated mayor requested the Queen's Own Rifles to come and disperse the strikers. Toronto newspapers, including the *Globe*, had kept the public hostile to the strike, and with predictable enthusiasm, the regiment was quickly assembled.

Based in the provincial capital, headquarters of businessmen who thought they stood to lose money by strikes, the Queen's Own Rifles was also largely composed of the sons of Toronto's elite, who had little sympathy for the working class and certainly none for sit-ins. On January 2, Henry Pellatt and the rest of the Queen's Own Rifles were rushed the 200 kilometres from Toronto to Belleville to quell "the riot", as Torontonians incorrectly called the strike. The government was in such a hurry that the militiamen were not issued proper winter clothing and some suffered from severe frostbite.

With fixed bayonets, the regiment marched against the snowball-hurling strikers and drove them from the Belleville rail yard to allow a train to leave for Montreal. "They acted with exemplary patience under the grossest provocation" was the *Globe*'s overblown praise. The newspaper fantasied that a mob 600 to 800 strong had defiantly hurled chunks of ice, bricks and bolts and that the Queen's Own Rifles were "insulted, spat upon and treated with every form of contumely without retorting or retaliating."

The railway and its workers settled their dispute the next day, and the Queen's Own Rifles returned home. As a souvenir of the occasion, courtesy of the Grand Trunk Railway Company, each man of the Queen's Own Rifles received a medal made from rail steel to commemorate "Belleville, 1877". Three years later, at the age of 21, Henry was made a lieutenant. The military was to become his most continuously successful and satisfying pastime.

Young Henry had joined the firm of Pellatt and Osler after he left school at 17, a common age for boys to start in business at that time. He maintained an active interest in sports and in the Queen's Own Rifles while he spent the next few years learning to be a stockbroker. By the time he was made a regimental captain in 1883, he was also a full partner in his father's business, now called Pellatt and Pellatt. A year earlier, Edmund Osler had left Pellatt Sr. to form Osler and Hammond, still a prominent Toronto brokerage house. An important part of the father and son business was to keep in contact with the commercial and industrial men of Toronto, and Henry's friendships with Upper Canada College graduates and his active participation in the Queen's Own Rifles gave him inside information about local business.

On June 15, 1882, Henry married Mary Dodgson, an English immigrant and a graduate of Toronto's exclusive Bishop Strachan School. The school had been established in 1867 and was operated by the Church of England—the religious affiliation of the Pellatts and of most of Toronto's social and financial leaders. Henry's parents were faithful parishioners of St. Peter's Church on Carleton Street and made donations to support Wycliffe Theological College. The marriage undoubtedly brought Henry contacts with important Toronto families that he might otherwise not have known.

Henry was hard-working, clever and ambitious and soon wanted to make a more substantial income than his commissions on stock sales. He could see that easy money was being made by clever stock promoters—those who made a business of forming companies, creating shares and then selling them—and confidently decided to try it himself. His earliest interest was electricity, then in its first stage of development.

Steam engines became commonplace after the 1820s, and gas lamps appeared on Toronto streets in the late 1840s. But in 1882, an American inventor, Thomas Edison, started an energy revolution by developing steam-generated electricity that could be transmitted over short distances to create artificial lighting. Henry, neither a scientist nor technician himself, foresaw that the technology of electricity would advance rapidly, and he intuitively knew that it could be profitable.

In 1883, having raised capital locally and in England, he formed the Toronto Electric Light Company and became its first secretary at a monthly salary of $25. Thus, at 24, Henry Pellatt had organized the first of many business ventures that would gain public confidence and attract investment capital. An unparalleled Canadian business career was underway.

His business venture, however, had small beginnings; the paid-up capital in the first year was only $175 000. The company imported and installed arc lights and produced steam-generated electricity to power them. The initial

Looking east along King Street E., near the turn of the century. The first street lights installed on this important downtown street were arc lights, which produced an intense light through the momentary contact of two rods of gas carbon. But arc lights were too brilliant and costly for use in homes and offices. Thomas Edison's invention of the smaller incandescent lamp eventually made electric lighting practical for domestic purposes. This light consisted of a carbon thread fastened to a pair of platinum wires and inserted into a glass bulb.

operation consisted of one 25-light and two 15-light generators in a building on Sherbourne south of Front Street. The first contract called for 32 arc lamps to be installed in hotels and large businesses in downtown Toronto. The next year, street lights were installed on Yonge, King and Queen Streets. In 1889, the Toronto Electric Light Company was incorporated and negotiated a 30-year monopoly on street lighting in the City of Toronto. By 1890, when the city's boundaries had been extended and the population had reached 181 215—an increase in one decade of 88 per cent—the company was providing power to arc lights on streets from West Toronto Junction to Woodbine in the city's east end. The light company expanded and relocated one block east of Yonge Street on the Esplanade.

Frederick Nicholls, an Englishman who had come to Canada in 1874, began to organize the Toronto Incandescent Electric Light Company in 1889 in an attempt to profit from additional advances in lighting technology. Realizing the potential of this new company, Pellatt became an investor, and in 1896, the two companies merged, retaining the name Toronto Electric Light Company. Even with its street lighting monopoly, the Toronto Electric Light Company did not pay a dividend to its shareholders from 1890 to 1899. In a financially sound and uncommonly foresighted manner, the shareholders allowed management to use profits to expand the company and improve technology. In 1891, however, shareholders received returns in the form of bonus issues of stock. One share was given for every two held.

Understanding both electricity and the stockbroking business, Henry was able to see the potential of another new invention: electrical locomotion. In 1885, Charles J. Van Depoele came from the United States to the Canadian Industrial Exhibition in Toronto—the forerunner of the Canadian National Exhibition—to give popular demonstrations of his new electric trolley-run railway. In Toronto, as in other North American cities, horse-drawn cars or sleighs transported the public. The innovative Van Depoele had hung an overhead wire conductor, attached a wheel to the end of a pole on the roof of a motorcar and then pressed the wheel upwards by means of a strong spring. When the wheel was in continuous contact with the overhead conductor, it would collect electric current and transmit it by means of another wire to the motor of the car. The motorcar, or trolley car as it was called, could then be propelled along metal tracks.

Pellatt, gazing out of the window of his father's brokerage office on King Street, watched a horse-drawn car amble slowly by. "Do you know, Father, that some day those streetcars won't need horses. They'll be driven by electricity." Many of the city elders thought Van Depoele's work merely a stunt or a gimmick, and Henry's father gave his opinion in no uncertain terms: "Sometimes, son, I think you're crazy!"

Though he could see the huge potential of electric locomotion, Henry was not yet wealthy enough to build electrical railways. This venture fell to William Mackenzie (1849-1923), a rising entrepreneur who would later organize the building of the Canadian Northern Railway, Canada's second transcontinental system. In 1891,

Mackenzie was able, as head of a four-man syndicate, to negotiate a 30-year monopoly with the City of Toronto for his new electric railway business. By 1893, its first full year of operation, the Toronto Electric Railway Company had gross earnings of $895 400—20 per cent more than the horse-drawn company's last full year of operation in 1890.

The implications were obvious to Henry Pellatt. His Toronto Electric Light Company provided electricity to power lights and machines. Why not railways as well? He began to buy as many shares of the Toronto Electric Railway as possible, not only as a show of confidence and to earn dividends, but also with hopes of eventually influencing company management.

One of Toronto's early electric streetcars on Davenport Road west of Bathurst Street, c. 1908

Monopolies and Speculation

Chapter 3

In 1892, Henry's father, known to his children as "the Governor", retired from the brokerage business to spend more time at his summer home on Lake Simcoe. It was rumoured within the Pellatt family that Henry had paid his father to retire. In any case, 33-year-old Henry became

Southwood, the retirement home of Henry Pellatt's father, near Orillia

sole director of Pellatt and Pellatt, and he was free to begin the wheeling and dealing that would, within the next two decades, make him dominate much of Toronto's social and economic life.

The Queen's Own Rifles appointed him major in 1893, and four years later, he was privileged to be part of the 300-man Canadian contingent at Queen Victoria's Diamond Jubilee. Pellatt mingled with the notables of Britain's far-flung colonies who had come to pay homage to the grand old monarch. He took part in pageants, parades, banquets and balls and loved every minute of it. To top it off, Henry was in command of the guard of honour during the impressive and colourful Thanksgiving service in St. Paul's Cathedral on May 24, Queen Victoria's birthday.

Pellatt's major success of the decade, however, involved not his glamorous military career, but the King Street financial world and the Canadian West. Canadians had promoted Confederation in 1867 in part to obtain control of the vast western regions of the continent—the modern provinces of British Columbia, Alberta, Saskatchewan and Manitoba. All this territory, except for what is now British Columbia, was purchased from the Hudson's Bay Company in 1868, but little use was made of it because of poor transportation and a series of economic depressions. The building of the Canadian Pacific Railway in the early 1880s briefly renewed public interest in the West. Businessmen promoted "get-rich-quick" schemes and stock deals in western land development. They incorporated land companies and sold stock at highly inflated prices to gullible city folk who believed settlement of the prairies was imminent. Henry Pellatt was witness to a typical stock-buying scene during Osler's last year in the Pellatt partnership.

The opening of Pellatt and Osler's public sale of Qu'Appelle Land Company stock on March 28, 1882 was a chaotic affair. By midday, when the sale was to begin, the brokerage front offices were completely jammed with impatient speculators. As the clock reached 12, the doors leading to the rear offices were opened and the crowd charged toward the desks where clerks were ready to receive subscriptions. Crash after crash was heard as glass partitions between the desks were broken by the jostling crowd. Buyers seemed to lose their senses as they fought to have their names registered first.

Scenes like this, outside a land office in Yorkton, Saskatchewan, were common during the 1880s and 1890s as land-hungry settlers and speculators struggled to be first in line to register land claims. The transcontinental railway did much to open the West to permanent settlement, but what were some of the other reasons for the late nineteenth-century migrations into the prairies?

Amid deafening shouts, excited buyers surrounded the clerks. The lone policeman present was powerless to control the crowd. As each investor managed to muscle his way to the stock book, others would seize him by the shoulders, arms and neck until someone would shout, "You are choking the man!" For a moment those behind would give their victim an opportunity to breathe. However, if he again attempted to register his name, he would be seized and dragged back, while those behind would clutch for the stock book. Before long it was in tatters. Some of the shouting crowd scrambled onto desks, chairs and counters. Pictures on the walls were ruined. It was impossible to go on with the sale, and finally more police arrived to force the mob outside.

Pellatt was impressed by this example of people's easily aroused greed. He was also aware of the realistic possibility of land development in the West, where he had travelled on the new transcontinental railway. Whenever he could afford to, Pellatt bought stock in the Canadian Pacific Railway and in the Northwest Land Company, a speculative operation that bought up townsites across the West in the hope that someday the rural farming population would be large enough to need and support towns and cities. Since western settlement was slow and difficult, most of Henry's peers thought that he should know better than to waste his money on stock that brought no immediate dividends and no guarantee of long-term success. But the pacification of native tribes and Métis people during the late 1880s and the prosperity of the 1890s brought, under the Laurier Liberal government of 1896-1911, an expansionary immigration policy. Cheap homesteads were promised to those willing to move to the Canadian West. Several hundred thousand land-hungry Europeans and Americans settled the land and built communities there. Profits of the Canadian Pacific Railway skyrocketed as people travelled across the continent by railway and grain was shipped to markets.

As immigration continued, land companies conducted clever advertising campaigns that exaggerated the potential of land sites and promised quick and easy fortunes for a few dollars invested. Easterners greedily bought land company stocks—which doubled and tripled in value—and rumours spread that Pellatt made three to four million dollars on his Northwest Land Company holdings, a figure that was probably highly inflated.

By this time, Henry was a wealthy young man and his personal reputation was above reproach, but his company, Pellatt and Pellatt, was deeply in debt to the Toronto-based Home Savings and Loan Company. In 1895, his company owed $226 375, and from 1898 to 1903, the debt rose from $389 130 to $955 124. Of course, this was not public knowledge, and Henry Pellatt was thought to be a model of success and affluence.

While the rural population of Canada increased by 600 000 from 1891-1911, the most noticeable growth occurred in the cities. Many farm youths migrated to urban areas to work in factories, and immigrants often stayed in the cities where they could live close to others who spoke their language. In 1891, only 1 537 098 Canadians lived in cities and towns, but by 1911, 3 272 947—almost half the total population—were city dwellers. The population of Ontario increased in this period by 412 971, and half that number went to Toronto, whose population more than doubled. The need for services such as electricity, which provided energy for transportation, homes and factories, grew accordingly. As a result, Henry Pellatt's stockbroking business flourished despite his debts, and his investments—especially in electricity—paid off.

With his new found wealth, Pellatt began to indulge in benevolent displays that made him a rarity in staid, conservative Toronto, where the rich were not in the habit of spending their money freely or giving it away publicly. In 1902, he began raising money for Trinity College in Toronto by asking his fellow citizens for donations and by

Lt.-Col. Henry Pellatt, 1901

personally pledging $25 000. He also furnished a mission church in Edmonton.

In 1903, Pellatt donated a complete set of modern surgical equipment to Grace Hospital in Toronto, then run by the Salvation Army. Henry was interested in "medical things" all his life. His niece Mary recalls:

> He aimed at one point to become a doctor. It was the days of apprenticeship and he was apprenticed to a doctor. He was supposed to be studying anatomy and, to get bones to study, he went to the Potter's Field, which was somewhere near Bloor and Yonge. He would bring bones home... and some of these bones weren't quite bare. So he put them in a big pot on the stove to stew.

It is obvious that, had Henry continued his medical studies, he would have been as adventurous and unusual in medicine as he was in finance.

When Pellatt made money, he did not simply put it into the bank to gather interest, but re-invested the funds in companies that he thought would return handsome profits. In 1901, for example, he and fellow financiers Mackenzie, Nicholls and Dominion Securities founder George Cox, obtained a 40-year monopoly in Brazil for an electric system, the Sao Paulo Tramway, Light and Power Company. A year later, Sao Paulo shares were quoted at $50, a 300 per cent increase since the company's incorporation. Two years later, with Sao Paulo a proven success, another Brazilian monopoly, the Rio de Janeiro Tramway, Light and Power Company, was formed. These two ventures merged in 1911 to form Brazilian Light and Traction—today known as Brascan—one of the few large Canadian-controlled multinational corporations.

Henry briefly thought of investing in the newly invented electric automobile. In the days before the harnessing of the internal combustion engine to the horseless carriage, many people, including Henry, thought that electric cars would be the coming thing. He went so far as to purchase the first such vehicle in Toronto. The story is told that one evening the uniformed Henry drove to a Queen's Own regimental drill at the Armories. But he couldn't stop the car! He was forced to keep it circling until some daring riflemen grabbed the car and forcibly steered it to a halt against the nearest wall. This incident dampened Pellatt's enthusiasm for electric cars.

Pellatt often invested other people's money. He borrowed freely from the Home Savings and Loan Company and from its successor, the Home Bank. In 1902, he was

The Toronto Armories, early 1900s. Queen's Own Rifles regimental drills were often held at this University Avenue location.

made a director of Manufacturers Life Insurance Company and chairman of its finance committee. Life insurance companies' assets grew rapidly in these prosperous years—from $83 million in 1890 to $163 million in 1910—and they were eager to invest this money. The 1906 Royal Commission on Insurance noted that Pellatt often personally determined the Manufacturers Life investments by purchasing securities without the finance committee's authorization and, furthermore, that he ensured that money was often invested in his own personal concerns. Apparently, this custom was commonplace in early twentieth-century business circles and not considered either immoral or illegal.

Pellatt encouraged the overlapping of interests for his own financial gain. In 1902-03, his interest in the Toronto Electric Railway Company brought results. Under Mackenzie's skilful management, the railway company's earnings had increased by 18.5 per cent each year. But electrical supply was dependent upon coal-fed steam generators. When strikes in Pennsylvania and British Columbia dragged on through the winter of 1902-03, the price of coal rose from $5 per ton in July to $10 in October when, in response to the emergency, it had to be imported from Wales. A cheaper energy source had to be found to ensure that the railway would continue to be profitable. Mackenzie saw that Pellatt and Nicholls, with their Toronto Electric

Light Company monopoly, could be partners to his own success; Henry was invited to become a director of the Toronto Electric Railway. All three knew that their businesses would need more and more electricity as they expanded, and now that alternating current was possible, they realized that electricity generated inexpensively at Niagara Falls and transmitted easily by hydro lines to Toronto could make fortunes for them. Coal would no longer be needed.

Two American companies were already generating electricity at Niagara Falls, but there was still room for one more. Despite vigorous promotional efforts by Niagara Falls authorities in previous years, no Canadian financier had been persuaded to invest money in hydro. The risk and cost were too high. Mackenzie, Pellatt and Nicholls shrewdly anticipated the enormous potential of electricity, and Pellatt correctly predicted: "We are on the eve of one of the greatest revolutions the world has ever known—a revolution which in its importance and far-reaching effect can be compared only with the invention of machinery and the discovery of steam power."

First, they purchased the rights to set up a generating plant from the Queen Victoria Niagara Falls Park Commission for $30 000. In February 1903, they incorporated the

Henry Pellatt (centre) laying one of the cornerstones at the site of the Electrical Development Company's Toronto Power plant, Niagara Falls

Electrical Development Company of Ontario with Pellatt as president, Nicholls as vice-president and general manager and Mackenzie as second vice-president. The stage was set for an interesting financial manoeuvre that was typical of the way these businessmen operated.

The Electrical Development Company was incorporated with a capital stock of $6 million, divided into 60 000 shares worth $100 each. The company then bought from the syndicate of Pellatt, Mackenzie and Nicholls their Niagara Falls rights for $6 million—$100 000 in cash and the balance in shares of capital stock of the company. To finance the construction of the hydro project, the syndicate agreed to raise $5 million from an issue of five per cent, 30-year bonds. Sixty two per cent of the bond issue was then taken up by the promoters themselves, their associates and companies they controlled. In effect, these three men invested only their original $30 000 and stood to make millions by selling their shares of capital stock when the public became confident that the scheme would be a success. This did not take long, since many prominent Ontario politicians, capitalists, manufacturers and retailers, impressed by the syndicate's reputation, jumped at the opportunity to become shareholders.

The Electrical Development Company was a link in a chain of companies that illustrates the phenomenon of vertical integration of business. Start with Mackenzie's Toronto Electric Railway Company. To guarantee a supply of electricity, the railway gained control of the Toronto Electric Light Company, first through an alliance with Pellatt and then, in 1911, by outright purchase of 99 per cent of the company's capital stock. To ensure a long-term generating capacity at a low rate, the Electrical Development Company was formed in 1903. To transmit the power to Toronto, a subsidiary, the Toronto-Niagara Power Company, was organized, and it acquired a right-of-way, 127 kilometres long and 25 metres wide at its narrowest, for its hydro transmission lines. All these companies were controlled by the same few men. It is also noteworthy that Nicholl's Canadian General Electric Company supplied the electro-hydraulic machinery at the Electrical Development Company's Niagara installations.

The Toronto Electric Railway Company was also monopolizing public transportation by acquiring competing companies—a process today called horizontal integration.

In 1906, the Mackenzie railway bought out another Pellatt, Cox and Nicholls interest, the Toronto and York Radial Railway System. It was an electric railway that ran north from Toronto, 50 kilometres up Yonge Street to Newmarket. Once purchased by the Toronto Railway Company, the line was extended north to Jackson's Point on Lake Simcoe and then east to Sutton. The railway system was almost 130 kilometres in length when completed and became a necessity for Torontonians who holidayed at Lake Simcoe in the days before the automobile became popular.

Much of the early success of Pellatt and his friends was due to the combination of talents the four men brought to the syndicate. Each was clever at raising money; each was willing to gamble on the industrial and commercial value of new technology; none hesitated to speculate with other people's investments; and each was an adventurer at heart. Cox, more than any of the others, had the financial connections through his control of the National Trust Company, Manufacturers Life Insurance Company and other insurance companies to borrow large amounts of capital. Nicholls was the most capable administrator; Mackenzie was skilful in manipulating politicians, and Pellatt was the "front man" with his public-spirited image. None of the four men was inclined to sit back and let American capitalists develop resource industry in Canada—they wanted power and profits for themselves.

Public Hostility Chapter 4

Of the 140 Canadians who held five or more directorates in the early 1900s, Nicholls and Cox headed the list with 28 each; Pellatt was tied for third place with 21. Their control of large corporations and apparent success in all their enterprises led to cries of monopoly and privateering. The public began to think that it was being victimized and accused Pellatt and his friends of charging unreasonably high transportation fares and electrical rates.

Small town businessmen wanted all electrical utilities brought under public ownership, for they understood that cheap electricity for the manufacturer would benefit entire communities. In 1901, they organized the Union of Canadian Municipalities to fight big-city monopolies and to lobby with government on behalf of towns, villages and small cities. This position was endorsed in 1903 by many Conservatives.

Pellatt and other capitalists had great business foresight, but they could neither measure the extent of public opposition to their schemes nor visualize the power that people could wield in union with government. Unwisely, the private electrical companies paid no attention to the municipalities and did nothing to quiet people's fears about monopolies. They refused to guarantee an inexpensive supply of electricity to the public or to manufacturers and insisted on maintaining high profit margins.

The Liberals had been in power in Ontario since 1873. In 1905, however, the Conservatives, under James Whitney, were elected, and the charismatic Adam Beck (1857-1925), a cigar-box manufacturer and former mayor of London, Ontario, was made a cabinet minister. He had already earned a reputation as an outspoken supporter of public ownership of electrical energy, and he immediately began to campaign on this issue within the government. As a direct result of Beck's lobbying, the Hydro Electric Commission of Ontario was set up in 1906 to initiate government participation in electricity production.

The debate over the merits of public versus private ownership intensified. The Union of Canadian Municipalities sponsored rallies and debates on the question. Beck

Adam Beck.
Why did he believe that the manufacture and distribution of hydro-electric power should be managed by government and not by private companies?

was a spellbinding speaker, and he drew large crowds wherever he went in Ontario. On one Saturday evening, 4000 people jammed into Toronto's Massey Hall to hear him argue passionately for public ownership of electrical utilities. Hardly a day went by without the controversy featured on the front page of the newspapers; the debate was on everyone's lips. The Toronto *World*, an outspoken opponent of the Electric Development Company, expressed the common belief that a publicly owned energy system would lower prices. There was a religious fervour to its charge: "The greatest light that God gave to man is the pure white light generated by God's greatest masterpiece—Niagara Falls. . . . Let us keep it forever for all the people, and let us put it in the house of every citizen, however humble, at cost price."

Pellatt, Mackenzie, Nicholls and their friends countered with speeches and public appeals of their own. The *Mail*, *Globe*, *News* and *Star* were all paid advertising rates for letters, articles and editorials favourable to the Electrical Development Company. The *World* was offered, and rejected, $350 000 to change its policy. Publication of these facts made people even more hostile.

The electrical syndicate went to great lengths to pressure the Ontario government into rejecting its public ownership policy. Eight per cent of direct foreign investment in Canada came from the United Kingdom, so a campaign was set up to influence important British investors and newspapers. Henry went to England since he was better known there than his partners. He claimed on behalf of the syndicate that public ownership of electricity was socialist, contrary to the spirit of free enterprise and a danger to private investors. Pellatt wanted influential Britons to withdraw their investments if the Ontario government continued with its public energy policy. The British responded favourably to the syndicate, but the Ontario government became even less patient with the Electrical Development Company promoters and went ahead with its own plans.

Mackenzie, Pellatt, Nicholls and Cox always tried to use other people's money for development projects. However, when tunnelling for the Electrical Development Company at Niagara Falls began in 1904, 38 per cent of the capital had yet to be raised by the sale of bonds. The company was still not in operation when the Conservatives gained power a year later. It then became almost impossible to sell bonds because the investing public refused to commit large sums for fear the government would take over the electrical monopoly.

To make sure that the facilities would be completed and a cheap energy source maintained for his railways, Mackenzie finally had to buy the Electric Development Company himself. This was accomplished in 1908 in a complicated manoeuvre whereby the Toronto and Mimico Railway, a subsidiary of the Toronto York Railway controlled by the Toronto Electric Railway Company, changed its name to the Toronto Power Company and then purchased the Electrical Development Company and the Toronto Niagara Power Company.

However, in 1910, when the Hydro Electric Commission started transmitting electricity from Niagara to Toronto in competition with the Electrical Development Company, there seemed little chance that the Pellatt-Mackenzie-Cox-Nicholls empire could last for long. Adam Beck, the "human dynamo", came out of the public ownership struggle a hero. Pellatt and friends were discredited and lost public sympathy. Pellatt himself sold out to Mackenzie in 1911 and turned his interests elsewhere. Private electrical companies were never again so profitable, and Mackenzie's Toronto-based companies were taken over by the municipal and provincial governments in 1921.

Crowds lined the festively decorated streets of Berlin (now Kitchener) to welcome the introduction of Ontario's publicly owned Hydro Electric Commission service, October 11, 1910.

Chapter 5 Personal Triumphs

By 1901, Henry Pellatt was a prominent military man; he was commanding officer, with the rank of lieutenant colonel, of the Queen's Own Rifles. During this year, the Duke and Duchess of Cornwall and York—the future King George V and Queen Mary—visited Toronto. In the largest militia parade ever held in the city, 11 000 men marched to the Exhibition grounds where the Duke, on a splendid white charger loaned to him by Pellatt, presented medals to veterans of the recent South African war. It was an auspicious occasion for Henry, because the Duke gave him a gold pin decorated with the York crest in diamonds and rubies, and for Canada, because this was the first time that the tune "O Canada" was performed publicly. It was played by the band during the Duke's inspection of the troops and, since it had been composed by a French-speaking Canadian, was intended as a tribute to Quebec.

In the spring of 1902, Pellatt was given command of the 657-soldier contingent that was to represent Canada at the coronation of King Edward VII in late June. In keeping with his increasing sense of philanthropy, Pellatt personally paid to equip the Queen's Own Rifles' band and to ship the group to England—all to spruce up Canada's image at the coronation. The contingent arrived in England in June and participated in a number of preliminary parades, but when the coronation was postponed six weeks because of the king's illness, the Canadians had to return home.

Almost 90 per cent of Toronto's population was of British descent. Most of these people were caught up in the glories of the British Empire, proud of their heritage and glad to be British subjects. Henry Pellatt himself was an avowed British imperialist. While some Canadians advocated an independent foreign and military policy, Pellatt spoke out for unity within the Empire. At a military banquet in March 1904, Pellatt declared:

Col. Sir Henry Pellatt in the regimental uniform of the Queen's Own Rifles, London, September 1910

The militia should be maintained at a sufficient strength and degree of efficiency to repel any sudden land attack against the Dominion. This force should be ready as volunteers to fight in any part of the world, side by side with the British regular. The future of Canada is inseparably bound up with that of Great Britain in a firm, loyal and immovable union.

In May 1905, Pellatt was appointed an aide-de-camp (A.D.C.) to Governor-General Earl Grey. In appointing Henry to this position, Grey wrote to the Prime Minister: "I have had the opportunity . . . to satisfy myself as to the smartness of the regiment under his [Pellatt's] command." Pellatt remained military aide to the king's representative in Canada during Grey's term of office and that of his successor, the Duke of Connaught.

Until 1921, when the practice was ended by the Canadian government, the British crown conferred knighthoods on Canadians nominated by the Governor-General of Canada. In 1905, the Laurier government arranged that

Henry Pellatt should be knighted by King Edward. Some have said, as did Sir Henry himself, that he was knighted for his work in electricity. (It can hardly be a coincidence that of the four main syndicate members, Cox and Nicholls became Senators and Pellatt and Mackenzie were knighted—all honours bestowed by the Laurier Liberal government.) But in fact, Pellatt's knighthood was a reward for his work with the Queen's Own Rifles.

The honour was engineered by Sir Frederick Borden, the Minister of Militia, and by Sir Wilfrid Laurier, who, according to Grey, "has twice approached me, the first time by letter, and subsequently at a private interview." Grey added: "The zeal and energy Sir Frederick Borden is displaying in his efforts . . . to place the militia on a thoroughly efficient and satisfactory basis make it desirable . . . to gratify his and Sir Wilfrid Laurier's desire on the subject of Colonel Pellatt."

It was at this time that Pellatt began to entertain lavishly; the entire Queen's Own Rifle bugle band, for example, was invited to celebrate New Year's day in 1906. This gala affair took place in Pellatt's Sherbourne Street mansion in Toronto's "classiest" residential area. New residential estates on the edges of the city such as Deer Park, Rosedale and Parkdale were being planned and were attracting the attention of the younger generation as popular places to live, but Pellatt had other ideas.

Steeped in family traditions, heraldry and British nobility, Henry was understandably fascinated by medieval knighthood. He collected and eventually donated a full collection of medieval weapons and armour to the Royal Ontario Museum. Castles fascinated him, and he dreamed of building his own. In the optimism and prosperity of the time, Pellatt made plans for Casa Loma—the "castle on the hill"—by buying a 10-hectare site on Wells Hill, an undeveloped area north of Toronto, south and east of present-day St. Clair Avenue and Bathurst Street. The castle was to be a magnet, a status symbol, the drawing card in a new, high-class land development scheme.

First, grand stables were built of Credit Valley cut stone. The horse stalls were made of Spanish mahogany and the walls of glazed tile imported from Spain. The floor tile was laid in a zig-zag pattern so the horses would not slip. Each horse's name was set in letters of 18-carat gold at the head of its stall, and modern, draught-proof windows

The extravagant stables at Casa Loma. Obviously, Henry Pellatt was fond of his horses. When his favourite white charger Prince suddenly lost its teeth, Pellatt had a set of dentures made to help the horse grind its food. Unfortunately, the false teeth did not work, and Pellatt eventually had to have the horse destroyed.

were included to protect the horses' health. Henry spent $250 000 building the elegant stables.

While the final plans for Casa Loma were being drawn up, Pellatt continued to spend much of his time with his regiment, for he was very proud of the militiamen and enjoyed being with them. He lavished money and attention on the Queens' Own Rifles, and largely because of his efforts, the Queen's Own had grown to two regiments by 1906.

In April of that year, Lieutenant-Colonel Pellatt took 891 men to New York City for a military tournament in Madison Square Gardens. The soldiers were described as "stunning" in their green uniforms with dark red trim and astrakhan caps. Pellatt boasted to the Toronto *World* of the efficiency with which the regiment boarded the train at Toronto en route to New York: "In just exactly four minutes from the time the first four in line struck the train the wheels were moving with every man allotted to the section in his place. The second section pulled out four and a half minutes after the first men entered the car."

The Canadians were highly praised for their splendid display, their marvelous marching and well-executed manoeuvres. The New York *Times* commented: "It appeared an impossibility for Lieutenant-Colonel Sir Henry

M. Pellatt to bring his 900 men into review formation but, by the most rapid and pretty soldierly manoeuvring, they were formed into battalions and marched past the reviewing officer."

Pellatt was rewarded for his efforts with a promotion to the rank of colonel, much to the dismay of many of the 150 officers with more seniority. A whirl of controversy flourished in militia circles. But Sir Henry's success was generally regarded as a reward for the prestige and popularity that his money had brought both to the Queen's Own Rifles and to the concept of a strong militia. Pellatt's crowning achievement came in 1910, the fiftieth anniversary of the Queen's Own Rifles. The British and Canadian governments announced that, at a personal cost of approximately $150 000, Sir Henry was planning to take 640 officers and men of the Queen's Own Rifles to England for army manoeuvres at Aldershot, a British military training centre.

Pellatt was glad not only to celebrate the anniversary, but also to impress the English-speaking world with his generosity—and no doubt to fulfill his own flamboyant ego as well:

The Queen's Own Rifles on their voyage to England, 1910

> I wish to mark the Jubilee year of the Queen's Own by some memorable event. The Queen's Own has given splendid service to Canada and to Toronto and deserves every recognition. The City of Toronto has always been proud of the regiment, and the Dominion of Canada has reason to congratulate itself upon the record of this most important unit.

But war clouds were on the horizon. Germany and Britain were at loggerheads over their world empires, and each was challenging the other to build bigger and better armies and navies. Pellatt, loyal to King and Empire, wanted to show how united Canadians were behind the British cause.

To warm up his regiment and the people of Toronto, Sir Henry staged an impressive Queen's Own Rifles reunion in the third week of June. It began with a Saturday garden party and reception in front of the Exhibition grandstand, attended by 10 000 people. Everyone who entered had to wear a uniform, and some guests even wore American military outfits. Eight men dressed as "Beefeaters" escorted Sir Henry and Lady Pellatt. The scene was colourful and impressive. Three bands played, 400 school children sang patriotic songs, and 30 native people performed a war dance. Sir Henry was then made a chief of the Six Nations and named Tanauyuasara, or Dawn of the Morning. The day was topped off by a "reunion smoker" in the Armories—presumably for men only—where 2500 guests celebrated into the evening.

On Sunday, a 3000-man parade was led by Pellatt and the Lieutenant-Governor up University Avenue to the front campus of the University of Toronto for open-air worship. The reunion celebrations continued during the week. Every evening from Monday to Thursday at the Canadian National Exhibition grandstand, a pageant was presented to show the role of the Queen's Own Rifles in Canadian history. The director of the Diamond Jubilee Parade in London was imported to plan and oversee these pageants. The participants were amateurs and many were members of the Queen's Own Rifles. Three hundred actresses were recruited by Lady Pellatt with the assistance of the International Order, Daughters of the Empire (I.O.D.E.), Queen's Own Rifles chapter, of which she was Regent.

The events were staged in front of impressive, oil-painted backdrop scenery, measuring 180 by 15 metres. The grand finale was the "Trooping of the Colour", presented by a combined regiment of Queen's Own Rifles, Royal Grenadiers and 48th Highlanders, and a living Union Jack—the flag of the Empire—formed by parading girls with their red, white and blue dresses gleaming under coloured lights. After the last performance, native people from the Brant reserve presented Sir Henry with an oil painting in appreciation for the opportunity he had given them during the pageant to act out their own interpretation of Canadian history.

A costume ball on Friday night capped the week's festivities. Three thousand took part in the opening procession. There were 15 different costume groups organized so that the march presented each group en masse, and the train of Lady Pellatt's gown was borne by two little boys dressed as sixteenth-century pages. The week-long celebration had been the spectacular creation of one man. Henry was enjoying his wealth and so were many Torontonians. The city had never seen the like before.

The Queen's Own Rifles left Levis, Quebec by boat for Liverpool on August 20. The weather was beautiful, and the regiment enjoyed the week-long voyage. One incident on the trip has been recorded. The officers won a tug-of-war

Men of the Second Regiment of the Queen's Own Rifles at Aldershot, England, 1910. Militia tradition required that soldiers' pay be "funded", i.e. turned back to the regiment to cover its expenses. Officers were also expected to provide their own uniforms. However, with the dedicated and generous Henry Pellatt leading them, men considered it a privilege to serve in the Queen's Own Rifles.

against the sergeants chiefly because the enormous Sir Henry, who now weighed 141 kilograms, was their anchorman. He had more than doubled his weight since his younger athletic days.

Most of September was occupied with marches and drills, mock battles and more marches, and the regiment saw much of southern England on foot. Unfortunately, eight officers, including Reg, Sir Henry's son, were stricken with typhoid fever. Lieutenant R. M. Gzowski died. One of those who survived the fever was Vincent Massey—son of a prominent Toronto family and another Upper Canada College graduate—who would become the country's first Canadian-born Governor-General.

The Queen's Own, led by the band of the Coldstream Guards, marched proudly through the streets of London on Saturday, September 17 to a civic reception given for the entire regiment by the mayor of London. Crowds of Britons, four to five deep, shouted "Good old Canadians" and "Bravo Queen's Own". The regiment arrived at the Guildhall to the music of "The Maple Leaf Forever". A seven-course meal and seven kinds of wine were served to the officers and men. In a stirring speech praising the Empire, Field Marshall Lord Roberts, the honorary colonel of the Queen's Own Rifles, said: "We must have one army inspired by the same feeling of comradeship and . . . common origin." Patriotically, Pellatt replied: "Canada and hundreds of thousands of such men as the Queen's Own are only too glad to respond to the first call whenever that call might come."

Later, the usually silent Pellatt was again called on to speak. Neither a profound thinker nor a particularly eloquent speaker, he gave a predictable address, which he had practised in the immense hall earlier in the afternoon. "The great object of our visit is . . . military education," explained Sir Henry. "It is to London and England that students flock, and why shouldn't the military come here to undergo, as it were, a postgraduate course in the great military centre of the Anglo-Saxon race." Loud cheers made Pellatt pause and then he went on, "The one great object was to show the home country exactly what can be counted on in the case of necessity." Resounding applause echoed the audience's agreement. Despite the evening's festivities, a Toronto newspaper proudly reported on the sobriety of the soldiers. "Not a man of the Queen's Own

The Queen's Own Rifles marched 20 kilometres through the "Metropolis of the Empire" on September 17, 1910. The military was a focus of public enthusiasm during the days of the British Empire. What part does military tradition play in Canadian society today?

fell out that night on the march back through London" to Chelsea Barracks where they slept.

Before the regiment returned to its military training, Sir Henry gave $12 spending money to each man. This gesture cost Pellatt $7200—a considerable sum to splurge. For Sir Henry himself this was a memorable time marked with prestige and honour. He dined with Empress Eugenie, the wife of Napoleon III of France and a close friend of Queen Victoria, and with members of the exclusive Savage Club. He inspected 7000 Boy Scouts, placed a wreath on General Wolfe's tomb and, of course, visited his hospitalized officers. In reward for this personal show of Empire solidarity and strength, King Edward presented Pellatt with the Commander of Victorian Order decoration at Balmoral Castle. He was now Sir Henry Pellatt C.V.O. These were the "golden days" of the Queen's Own Rifles—largely at Henry Pellatt's expense.

Castle on the Hill Chapter 6

Most years, it seems, Sir Henry found time amid his financial dealings to tour parts of Europe. During his trips, Pellatt visited many old castles and formed an image of the one he would one day construct. "Casa Loma," Sir Henry once commented, "is a result of my observations and travels." And the "castle on the hill" certainly proved to be an extraordinary blend of Pellatt's experiences. He built the castle exactly the way he pleased. It was not a cold, damp, draughty medieval castle but a modern and up-to-date spectacle dressed in old-fashioned architecture. From the outside it appeared built of stone; in reality, it was constructed with steel-reinforced concrete and faced with stone. Pellatt combined his love of grandeur, tradition and knighthood with his fascination for technology and modern convenience. And by the time the four years of construction ended in 1914, Casa Loma had cost Sir Henry about $3.5 million.

Casa Loma had 98 rooms, three bowling alleys, 30 bathrooms—but only 15 baths (some with gold-plated fixtures)—25 fireplaces, telephones, a built-in vacuum system, a huge fountain, a kitchen stove large enough to cook a whole steer and 5000 electric lights. It was the only castle in the world that could boast an electrically operated elevator and an indoor swimming pool. There was a 50-metre shooting gallery and, deep in the basement, stood the greatest wine cellar on the continent, with 1700 temperature-controlled cavities for wine bottles. An underground tunnel 244 metres long and 5.5 metres beneath the road connected the castle basement to the stables. To heat the massive buildings the large underground furnace burned 725 metric tons of coal a year.

Immediately inside the main entrance off Austin Terrace was the great hall with a beamed ceiling 18 metres high, a $75 000 pipe organ and a throne modelled on the one in Westminster Abbey where British kings and queens are seated for their coronations. Just west of the hall was a solid, oak-panelled drawing room that took three European artisans three years to produce. The floor was laid in a variation of parquet design cemented on a cloth base so

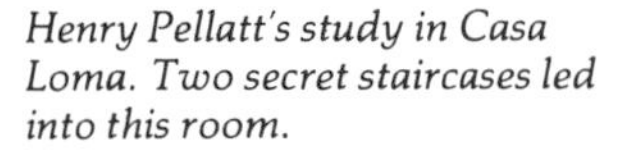

Henry Pellatt's study in Casa Loma. Two secret staircases led into this room.

that not a single nail was needed. Pellatt's library, housing his 100 000 books, was to the east of the great hall and featured a floor of Canadian oak and an elaborate ceiling with the Pellatt coat of arms moulded into the plaster.

Another highlight of the castle's construction was a first floor hall, a replica of one in Windsor Castle, called Peacock Alley. It had very expensive Burmese teak flooring, six centimetres thick, which was secured and held together by mahogany strips and rosewood wedges rather than nails. Pellatt's study had two secret exits concealed in the wall panelling; one stairway lead up to the second floor, the other down to the vault. The shower off Sir Henry's bedroom was constructed so that he could control

Peacock Alley, a first-floor hallway in Casa Loma

the water coming at him from all directions without having to turn around.

Pellatt furnished his home with costly treasures from all over the world. His motto seemed to be "The bigger, the better." He had a collection of English mantels—the cheapest cost $1800 and the most expensive, $12 000. He brought back Chinese vases, European tapestries, silver, rugs, paintings and furniture. There is a story told about two workmen at the castle installing a huge chandelier. They were having difficulty hanging it from the ceiling, and just as Lady Pellatt walked into the room, the enormous fixture crashed to the floor and broke into thousands of pieces. There was an embarrassed silence, and then

Guests in the Palm Room, c. 1914

Lady Pellatt turned to the men and said, "Never mind, we'll just order another one."

Everything about Casa Loma was done on a grand scale. Pellatt even imported Welsh and Scottish stonemasons, reputedly the best in the world. Not only were the castle walls fashioned by these experts, but Sir Henry, at a dollar a stone, had the castle surrounded by a wall that cost a quarter of a million dollars.

The superintendent of Casa Loma employed at least two full-time gardeners to maintain the well-groomed appearance of the 10-hectare estate. There were over 400 varieties of trees, shrubs and plants from around the world. On the east end of Casa Loma was a marble conservatory, entered through solid bronze Italian door frames, then worth $10 000 each, and illuminated by sunlight that streamed through the grapevine design of the conservatory's $10 000 stained glass dome. Large flower beds along the sides of this room were kept warm by a steam pipe system and displayed exotic and rare species. Pellatt often entered his flowers in horticultural competitions and won many prizes.

Sir Henry delighted in watching his utopia arise on Wells Hill. He was a kindly man and not a steel-hearted "captain of industry" like some of his peers. He would often provide a chicken or sack of oranges or box of chocolates for the men working on his showplace home and, on his own initiative, arranged and paid for the funerals of the brother and wife of George Thompson, his head gardener.

Sir Henry and Lady Pellatt took an interest in all kinds of people and thought nothing of entertaining thousands of guests at castle parties. Sometimes Sir Henry would invite the Queen's Own Rifles up for a weekend visit, and a thousand troops would be quartered in Casa Loma's basement. One grand occasion was a visit by the Duchess of Devonshire on May 28, 1921, when she presented the highest award of the Girl Guides, the Silver Fish, to Lady Pellatt for her nine years of work as Canadian Girl Guide Commissioner. This event was attended by hundreds of Guides, the Governor-General and Canon Cody, rector of St. Paul's Church on Bloor Street and chancellor of the University of Toronto.

The Pellatts also held parties for their staff. George Thompson's son Tommy recalls:

> They used to take place in the library. Lady Pellatt and Sir Henry too; they were royalists, monarchists, and proud, proud. They had a fellow named Dawson. He sang a parody to the tune of "God Save the King", and the words he used were: "Oh what a fool am I, Gosh what a fool am I, Oh what a fool." Upon hearing the strains of the national anthem, Lady Pellatt stood up at attention and stayed there all through Dawson's piece, notwithstanding the words . . . which demonstrates her allegiance. It shows a dedication almost unknown today.

Henry Pellatt loved display and ceremony. He would strut through the grounds of Casa Loma with great pomposity—head held high, hands linked behind his back and whistling at a high pitch through his teeth. The castle was his extravaganza, his spectacular production. One architectural critic described it as "a mixture of 17th century Scotch baronial and 20th Century Fox". Another considered it "unique and irreplaceable, a significant cultural document of the first order". Henry liked to think it embodied the best of a magnificent castle on the Rhine and a millionaire's home in Denver, Colorado.

Chapter 7 Pinnacle of Power

In the years immediately before World War I, Henry Pellatt was at the height of his career. When he sold the Toronto Electric Light Company to the Toronto Electric Railway Company in 1911, he had made a fortune and spent much of it building his castle. He had cultivated a deserved reputation as a gentleman and a philanthropist—his latest gift was a $155 000 building in England called Clifford's Inn, which was to be used as headquarters for the Society of Knights Bachelor. By the age of 52, he had achieved athletic, military and financial success, and Casa Loma gave him great personal satisfaction and unparalleled status in the eyes of most Torontonians. However, many of the established, wealthy families of Toronto considered him eccentric, if not a fool, for spending his fortune on buildings and showy affairs.

Mackenzie King, Lady Pellatt and Sir Henry Pellatt at King City, c. 1911

Nevertheless, Sir Henry was a member of all the important Toronto clubs. The York Club, the conservative Albany Club for businessmen and the Toronto Club, founded in 1835 and still the most exclusive in the country, were all open to him. In Ottawa, Pellatt belonged to the Rideau Club, which had been founded in 1865 by John A. Macdonald. Henry was particularly interested in the St. George's Society, which met yearly on April 23rd to commemorate the patron saint of England.

Pellatt was a communicant of St. James Cathedral, a church that had been destroyed by fires and rebuilt several times during the previous century. Its spire, nearly 100 metres high, made it the tallest building in North America at the turn of the century. The Church of England in Canada was important to Henry Pellatt throughout his life. Its traditions and ceremony appealed to him and provided a spiritual link to his English ancestors and the British Empire. The church also reinforced his sense of duty.

The welfare of his family, especially his brothers who had fared less well than he under the "Governor's" domineering influence, was a continuing responsibility for Sir Henry. He helped his youngest brother Mill become the paymaster at the Toronto Electric Light Company and promoted his marriage to a Miss Bannerman, nurse to the ailing Pellatt Sr. Henry set up another brother Fred, who had been a prisoner of war in South Africa and never fully recovered his health, on a farm near Orillia. Duty demanded that Fred's boys be boarded and educated at Ridley College after the breakdown of their parents' marriage and that Mary, Mill Pellatt's only child and Sir Henry's goddaughter, be given the opportunity to attend Bishop Strachan School and Trinity College. Henry was executor of his father's estate and, after the senior Pellatt's death in 1909, was responsible for trust funds left to help the wider family in times of need. But none of his family, other than his wife Mary, figured prominently in Henry's business or social life. His niece Mary explains:

> My father was so much younger than Sir Henry, and my mother had no use for anything to do with drink. We weren't exactly the poor relations, but we stayed outside the social aura. It was really only after he'd lost most of his money and a good many friends with it and was getting older and had outlived a fair number that we had a much closer contact.

In June 1911, Sir Henry and his wife were present at the coronation of King George V. At his own expense, Pellatt had commemorative medallions minted and presented to all the school children in Toronto. In this same year, he was elected president of the English Society of Knights Bachelor. Pellatt liked to brag about the time he made a special voyage to England for lunch with the Society and then sailed for Canada immediately after eating.

On May 9, 1912, the University of King's College in Windsor, Nova Scotia conferred an honorary doctor of civil law (D.C.L.) degree upon Sir Henry. He always joked among the family that D.C.L. stood for "darn crazy lunatic". Nevertheless, he must have been pleased with the honour, for he had a portrait painted of himself wearing academic robes, and in 1914 he returned the favour and endowed the chair of philosophy at King's.

Sir Henry Pellatt and his son Reg, 1911

In 1911, Henry made an unusual public foray into politics. His only other political involvement had been in 1902 when he spoke out against a prohibition referendum on grounds that it would force drinking from "licensed and regulated places to unlicensed and disreputable resorts and to the homes of people." Pellatt was outraged to hear Laurier's Liberals campaign on a platform of reciprocal free trade with the United States and the building of a navy independent of Great Britain, for he was convinced that a strongly unified British Empire should stand against the world. Consequently, Sir Henry donated £500 to an English fund to promote imperial trade preferences and tariffs in opposition to American free trade. He also placed a private railway car at the disposal of the Rt. Hon. Walter H. Long, a British Member of Parliament, who toured Canada promoting the Empire. Pellatt and his wife accompanied Long and the British party on most of the western trip and were delighted to know that their influence helped to defeat the Liberals.

Why were many Canadian businessmen like Pellatt opposed to free trade with the United States in 1911?

By this time, Henry was well-known by the British government and the royal family as a staunch supporter of the crown and the British imperialist cause. He received special attention from the Governor-General, the Duke of Connaught, who went on a moose-hunting expedition northwest of Sudbury and stayed at a lodge owned by Pellatt. Henry also escorted the Governor-General on a tour of the Niagara fruit belt. In return, Sir Henry gladly donated $5000 to a fund for the Victorian Order of Nurses, which the Duke was sponsoring.

As two of Toronto's most prominent citizens, Pellatt and his wife were often the subject of newspaper and magazine social notes and gossip columns. For many years, Sir Henry kept a collection of newspaper cartoons in which he was portrayed—often in an uncomplimentary way. In one interview, Sir Henry was asked about his former athletic prowess and his present physical condition. (Although he diligently weighed himself every day, his girth prevented him from seeing his feet.) Pellatt claimed that, at 54, he still "worked out" three times a week in a private gymnasium before going to the office. "I put on my trunks, go through extension exercises, use the horizontal bar, run a little and then submit to a rub-down." Uncharacteristically, he then gave a pep talk on the value of such self-discipline: "If men only knew what systematic exercises would do for them in clearing brains and keeping them physically fit, there wouldn't be gymnasiums enough in town to accommodate the applicants."

Pellatt credited much of his "good' physical condition to the long walks he took through Casa Loma, the conservatory, the stables and the gardens. On weekends he rode horseback on his recently purchased 600-hectare model farm at King, north of Toronto. Here he kept pheasants and a large herd of elk and deer, a number of which had been sent to him by King George V from his Windsor castle estate. The son of one of the gardeners recalls that Pellatt's horseback riding consisted of the "master" dozing in the saddle and the horse finding the way home. Certainly Pellatt liked his naps. "I know that I am always ready for bed at ten o'clock," Sir Henry revealed to a newspaper reporter. "I am a firm believer in the old adage about early to bed and early to rise. Nothing helps more to keep a man in good physical trim." Pellatt also had a ravenous appetite but was anxious not to appear a glutton in public. After entertaining guests for dinner, Sir Henry would often eat another meal alone.

Whatever his physical condition, Pellatt remained extremely active and successful in business and finance. To help ensure a cheap supply of fuel for his generators in the early days of electricity, Pellatt had invested heavily in coal mining. However, since electricity and public transportation were going to be taken over by government, he began to invest more money in mining and mineral-processing industries. He was a director of the Dominion Steel Corporation, West Dome Mining Company and McIntyre Mines Limited, as well as founder and first president of the Cobalt Lake Mining Company.

Pellatt's mining success—he became president of the Mining Corporation of Canada in 1916—was balanced by resounding failure in oil. He promoted a stock scheme called La Paz Oil, which won him notoriety when the company had to declare bankruptcy. Most employees at Casa Loma, confident of Sir Henry's financial reputation, had bought La Paz shares and subsequently lost their investment.

Entrepreneurs like Pellatt realized that in the cut-throat world of business competition only companies using the latest technology and machinery could produce goods cheaply and quickly. Small companies stood little chance against big ones. Pellatt was involved in many mergers of small, independent operations into large conglomerates. He was a founder of the British Columbia Packer's Association, the British-Canadian Shipbuilding and Dock Company at Sydney, Nova Scotia and a director of the Dominion Iron and Steel Company (now DOFASCO). Each of these companies shut down operations within their organization that were inefficient and technologically outmoded and centralized production to take advantage of transportation to markets and cheap labour. Consequently, the operations would often specialize in only one aspect of production at any one location. This was the forerunner of modern multinational corporations. Today, these companies may extract a mineral in one country, ship it to another for processing and then sell the finished product around the world.

Pellatt had many other business interests. Influenced by William Mackenzie, he had been one of the incorporators of the Grand Trunk Railway. In 1914, he became founder and first president of the Empire Life Insurance Company. He was also a director of the Western Assurance Company, the British American Assurance Company, Page Hersey Tubes, the Richelieu and Ontario Navigation Company and Canada Steamship Lines. But despite his financial status and respectability, Pellatt was still not ready to retire. Perhaps in an attempt to duplicate his youthful success in the Northwest Land Company, he plunged into another land speculation venture.

Chapter 8 Financial Disaster

Even at his most romantic and fanciful times, Pellatt was a financier out to make a quick dollar. At an age in life when most men become content to live with the memory of past glories and to take few chances, Pellatt, with all the tricks of the Toronto financial world at his command, plunged onward. Casa Loma had eaten into his personal fortune, and he turned to land deals to recoup his money.

In 1911 and 1912, Pellatt incorporated three land companies: Home City Estates, Toronto City Estates and British Colonial Land and Securities. Although these companies also bought land near Hamilton and St. Catharines, they concentrated on land speculation in and around Toronto, especially in the area of Casa Loma. Pellatt had plans for a large, high-class subdivision to be called Cedarvale in the St. Clair, Bathurst, Vaughan Road area, to which Torontonians would flock to buy land and build homes because of the presence of Casa Loma.

The establishment of Home City Estates was typical of all these land companies. On January 31, 1912, Sir Henry

Pellatt hoped that an exclusive neighbourhood would grow up around his "castle on the hill".

purchased a farm on the outskirts of Toronto for $321 192.29. $121 192.29 was paid in cash, and the person selling the property agreed to take back a $200 000 mortgage. On February 24, Home City Estates was incorporated, and on March 19, Pellatt sold the property to Home City for $1 205 000—$205 000 in cash plus the $200 000 mortgage assumed by the company, $200 000 at six and one-half per cent interest to be paid in six months to Pellatt and $600 000 worth of company stock. On paper at least, Pellatt had made a profit of $889 000—a deal similar to the organization of the Electrical Development Company six years earlier.

Why did he inflate the land value so much? If enough people could be convinced that Home City held lands worth over a million dollars, shares would be in demand, and whether Henry sold any land or not, he could make money on the stock market. Either way, he thought he couldn't lose. A stock gambler and adventurer since his youth, the absence of ready capital was not an obstacle to his plans. Pellatt had always borrowed heavily from banks and was never known to have welched on a debt. The Home Bank, successor since 1905 to the Home Savings and Loan Company, to which Pellatt and Pellatt had been deeply in debt for years, supported Sir Henry's land development schemes. Pellatt and Pellatt's loan balance varied yearly from $600 000 to over a million dollars.

During World War I, however, Canadians put their money into war bonds and industries that would benefit from wartime production, such as munitions and uniforms. People did not buy land and did not build houses. The land development companies, therefore, held lands that no one wanted. During this period, Pellatt was not able to pay the interest on the amount owed by his stockbroking company to the Home Bank. Each year the interest owing was added to the principal outstanding and his debts grew larger and larger. The bank did not force Pellatt to sell his land holdings to pay his debts. Instead, it loaned him more money! Further complicating the problem was the bank's policy to take land company stock as collateral on the loans. Deeply involved in these dealings were three Home Bank officials, all friends and business associates of Henry Pellatt.

In 1921, when Pellatt's financial position still had not improved, the bank finally hired the Chartered Trust

Company's real estate division to investigate Pellatt's land companies. On April 20, 1921, the Chartered Trust reported that Sir Henry and W.J. Rooney, a recent partner in Pellatt and Pellatt, both managers of Toronto City Estates, were no longer fit to manage company affairs. In somewhat gentle terms, it said that management must be placed with someone "who is more familiar with the details of the real estate business. . . . If the company is allowed to go along in its present condition, there is no outlook for it but bankruptcy. A vigorous house-cleaning is necessary."

More damaging was the Chartered Trust's comments on the landholdings themselves. A Dawes Road property was said by Toronto City Estates to be worth $722 712.30, but the trust company evaluation showed that it was worth only $145 474. This was typical of the Pellatt properties. Not only had they increased little in value since his vast pre-war speculations, but most lots remained unsold. The trust company commented that Pellatt had imposed high property restrictions on his lands in keeping with his ideas of the class of people he wanted as neighbours. But, said the Chartered Trust Company, Cedarvale was surrounded by the homes of lower- and middle-class workers. Pellatt's restrictions were also a mistake because the subdivisions of Rosedale, Avenue Road Hill, Moore Park, North Toronto and Chaplin Estates were all in competition for the same buyers.

Toronto's population had reached 521 893, an increase of 40 per cent in 10 years. While Pellatt was building his castle, thousands of new Torontonians were jammed together downtown in shacks with primitive sanitation and heating facilities. Toronto's assistant relief officer had noted that "there is scarcely a house fit to live in that is not inhabited by numerous families; in fact, respectable people have had to live in stables, tents, old cars, sheds, in damp cellars, where we would not place a valued animal, let alone a human being." A younger Pellatt might have seen the need for low-cost housing and adapted his companies to that market. Sir Henry, however, was unable to give up his dreams for Cedarvale.

Pellatt's failure to sell land meant that the stocks the bank owned in Sir Henry's land companies were worthless. Bank officials realized that they had little chance to regain the money Pellatt owed. Accountant G.T. Clarkson reported to the bank's general manager, J. Cooper Mason,

The corner of Yonge and Queen Streets during the 1920 streetcar strike. As Pellatt and other wealthy people built spacious and lavish homes on the outskirts, downtown Toronto grew steadily more congested. The housing shortage was often acute, and people, many of them recently arrived from Europe or rural Canada, had to learn to live in the cramped quarters of a modern city.

on April 20, 1923 that "the affairs of Pellatt and Pellatt and Sir Henry Pellatt are in a mess" and that "the possibility of the bank recovering anything from such assets is very greatly outweighed by the embarrassment which would come to it if Pellatt and Pellatt should be forced into bankruptcy."

The Home Bank was in a difficult situation. Even if it wanted to take over Pellatt's properties to pay his debts, a great public loss of confidence in the bank would occur when it was discovered that the institution had not taken proper precautions to protect its loans. Pellatt stayed calm amid all these troubles, and according to Frederick Griffin, Pellatt's first biographer, Sir Henry even managed to fall asleep during a lengthy meeting of the bank's directors, designed to question him about his account. Pellatt's banking problem was resolved, after a fashion, on August 17,

1923, when the Home Bank declared bankruptcy. Later investigations into Home Bank affairs revealed a side of Sir Henry's career that the public had never suspected.

The Home Bank was begun in Toronto in the 1850s when Bishop Charbonelle used savings entrusted to him by Irish immigrants to establish the Toronto Savings Bank. In the beginning it opened only on Saturdays so that working-class people could do their banking on their half day off. From there it developed into the Home Bank—a 63-branch operation across Canada by the 1920s. The bank's 60 000 depositors were people of modest income and included many small town residents.

The Home Bank was the ninth—and last—Canadian bank since Confederation to declare bankruptcy. Its debts of $18 486 978 were larger than any failed bank since 1868. A subsequent royal commission uncovered evidence of gross mismanagement, and after the commission's interim report in June 1924, the bank's directors and officials were arrested. They were eventually tried and convicted of conspiracy and of filing false returns. They won an appeal, however, and never served their sentences.

The appeal decision was somewhat of a whitewash, considering the practices uncovered by the commission. For a number of years, the bank had been paying yearly dividends to shareholders out of deposits rather than profits. In 1916, for example, when a profit of $133 406 was shown by the bank's yearly statement, uncollected interest to the amount of $210 000 had been put into the profit account. By the end of 1918, the accumulated and unpaid interest on bank loans totaled $676 000.

The bank's officials seem to have been desperate to hide the true situation from shareholders and depositors. By declaring a yearly dividend, public confidence was maintained in the bank despite the occasional rumours that things were not well. During the war, the western directors of the bank had asked the Minister of Finance to check into the bank's practices, but he did not want to risk a run on a bank during wartime, when financial and political stability seemed so important. He merely asked that the bank reorganize its directorate.

Other irregularities were discovered. The bank's employees were underpaid, but when they asked for wage increases, the management felt incapable of paying them and encouraged them to overdraw their accounts instead.

The overdrafts were then declared assets in the bank's yearly statements, and no charge was made to the expense side of the ledger to reduce the so-called profits. Eventually, $100 595 was overdrawn in this manner.

At the time of bankruptcy, the bank had three large debtors. Pellatt and Pellatt owed $1.7 million; A.C. Frost, a British Columbia timber concern controlled by Americans, $1.8 million; and the Prudential Trust Company, $1 million. All had failed to make interest payments. The deeper these companies went into debt, the more the bank felt it had to support them for fear that they would go bankrupt and ruin the bank.

H.J. Daly, president and ex-director of the bank, also turned out to be vice-president of the A.C. Frost Company. While conflict of interest was not illegal at that time, there clearly seemed to have been a lack of moral judgement. Furthermore, the commission discovered that bank officials had manipulated the bank's funds in order to buy Sir Henry Pellatt 432 shares of the bank's stock.

Testimony during commission hearings in April and May 1924 often revolved around Sir Henry. One prominent witness, federal Minister of Finance Sir Thomas White, when questioned about Pellatt's business practices, reported:

> Sir Henry Pellatt built, upon the foundation laid by his father, one of the largest brokerage businesses in the Dominion of Canada and, ever since I can remember, has borrowed from banks and financial institutions and has met his obligations. . . . Sir Henry was reputed to be a very wealthy man. A man who builds a million dollar house, in the minds of the public, is presumably a man who is well to do.

Pellatt had developed this safe, respectable image to add to his borrowing power and to encourage others to invest with him and to trust his ideas and plans. He was so successful that his creditors didn't realize until it was too late that he needed to reduce expenses and begin paying his debts. But the public, though they were informed of his possible part in the Home Bank failure, soon forgot all that in favour of the flamboyant Pellatt of Casa Loma and the Queen's Own Rifles.

Sir Henry Pellatt in one of his more elaborate costumes

Chapter 9 The Last Hurrah

The collapse of the Home Bank shattered many lives. Depositors received only 25 per cent of their money; those who had accounts of less than $500 were given a further 37 cents on the dollar two years after the bank's closing. Others suffered more severely. J. Cooper Mason, the bank's general manager, died two weeks before the bank failed; H.J. Daly, the president, passed away the day before the royal commission's interim report was issued. In April 1924, Henry's wife, Mary, died after a heart attack. The *Globe*'s obituary headline read, "Lady Pellatt dies of sudden illness. Woman of high attainments, widely known and admired, is no more."

Sir Henry was short of money and the expense of running the castle was draining him. It took more than 40 servants to maintain it at a cost of $22 000 a year. Fuel alone cost $15 000. From the castle's early days, Sir Henry had battled municipal authorities over property taxes, and despite his lawyers' best efforts, the taxes rose every year to a high of $12 000. By 1924, Henry, weary of the expense and struggle, turned Casa Loma over to the city and moved to a large apartment on nearby Spadina Road.

So desperate was Pellatt for funds that most of his Casa Loma art treasures were auctioned at a gigantic sale held over several days in June 1924. Dealers from across the continent jammed into the castle's conservatory, filling every chair, lining the walls and packing the doorways. "It is a sale which breaks my heart," Sir Henry confided to a Toronto *Star* reporter. The *Evening Telegram* ran bold headlines proclaiming, "Art connoisseurs reap golden opportunities" and "Sumptuous offerings from Casa Loma's store of treasures dazzle bidders."

A half dozen solid silver tea services, crystal goblets, a Chinese incense burner, a Bohemian glass flower stand, antique English ale glasses, a Louis XVI chest and an Imperial Japanese cloisonné vase were only a fraction of the collection that fell under the auctioneer's hammer. Five early George II solid silver spoons and a gravy ladle, hallmarked 1759 and once the property of Governor Simcoe, were bought by a Detroit man for $28. An eight-day

The Casa Loma library housed a few of the treasures in Henry Pellatt's $1.5 million art collection.

grandfather clock with a calendar in a Chippendale mahogany case with brass and silver engraved dials was purchased for $125. One of the prize offerings was "The Shepherdess", the last known painting by Canadian Paul Peel. The items that were auctioned were listed in the newspapers and, set in small type, covered two complete pages.

The spectators gasped as article after article was brought forward for inspection and sale by the auctioneer. It was one of the best public entertainments Toronto had offered since the great fire of 1904 destroyed most of the downtown business section. Proceeds of the sale amounted to $250 000. It was a tragic end for a $1.5 million collection.

Although no one has lived in Casa Loma since, there have been a number of attempts to use it. Initially, rumours spread that the federal government might purchase it as a home for war veterans. Toronto-born Hollywood actress Mary Pickford considered it as a setting for several movies. There were proposals that it be made into a high school, a convent and an Orange Lodge. In 1928-29, an attempt was made to run it as an apartment hotel. A syndicate spent $250 000 on renovations, but the Depression ended their hopes. Their ambitions were too lofty in any case: it is said that the $10 000-a-year chef used to arrive for work every day wearing a top hat and driven in a chauffeured limousine. During World War II, the stable and carriage house were used by an engineering company to assemble sonic apparatus used to detect German submarines.

In 1936, the Kiwanis Club of West Toronto began to renovate and operate Casa Loma as a tourist attraction, leasing it from the city for a percentage of the admission charge. Four hundred thousand tourists now pass through the castle halls every year. Many formal dances, weddings and receptions are also held there, and the third floor has been turned into a Queen's Own Rifles museum. Proceeds from the public use of Casa Loma go towards youth programs, the Kiwanis Music Festival, volunteer service work with the mentally ill, educational funds and scholarships, child aid and other worthy causes. Since 1936, $1.5 million have been raised.

Less than a year after the auction, Henry, now 66 years of age, retired from the brokerage business. Pellatt and Pellatt was left in the hands of his only son, Reg, and two partners, Norman Macrae and William Rooney. During the Depression, Henry gave much of his own depleted resources to his son to help him survive in the stockbroking business.

This group of Toronto school girls were early visitors to Casa Loma.

A memorable occasion during Sir Henry's retirement years was a party held at his King estate in June 1926 to celebrate his 50-year association with the Queen's Own Rifles. After his retirement from active command in 1911, Pellatt had been made honorary colonel, a distinction he treasured. In 1921, he had reached the rank of major general. Highlighting the party was a detachment of the East Kent Regiment of Buffs, a famous British outfit that had been associated with the Queen's Own Rifles on their trip to England in 1910, and the presentation of a ceremonial sword to Pellatt in front of the nearly 2000 spectators who lined the shores of Mary Lake, named by Pellatt for his wife. The Lieutenant-Governor, Colonel Harry Cockshutt, made the presentation:

It gives me great pleasure to present this ceremonial sword to one whose service to the Dominion has been so very commendable. While peace now reigns within our borders, we hope that all men may show the same devotion to their country which you have shown in the past.

Representatives of many organizations with which Sir Henry had been associated in the past 50 years were on hand to honour him. Presentations were made on behalf of both the National Chorus, which Pellatt had supported for 15 years, and the St. John's Ambulance Brigade, which he had organized in Canada and served as commissioner. Although too old for active service during the war, Pellatt had acted as a brigadier general in charge of the Toronto Infantry Brigade and had helped the Red Cross and the Order of St. John to train voluntary detachments of nurses for work at the European fronts. Hundreds of parcels containing food and clothes were sent to Queen's Own Rifles prisoners of war in Germany via an association formed by Henry Pellatt. He was also a commissioner of the federal military hospital commission, formed to ensure the best possible treatment for wounded and maimed soldiers.

Sir Henry replied to the presentations using the regiment's motto, "In peace prepared", as his theme. He spoke of his mission in 1910 and of his attempt to keep his regiment ready for the war that had seemed inevitable. While he spoke, a stunt squadron of three airplanes performed overhead. After the National Chorus sang, 500 members of the Queen's Own Rifles, commanded by Colonel Reg Pellatt D.S.O., O.C., marched in review. Sir Henry was very pleased.

In 1927, Pellatt married a life-long friend, Catherine

Sir Henry and the second Lady Pellatt at their Mary Lake farm, c. 1929

Welland Merritt. She was a granddaughter of William Hamilton Merritt of St. Catharines, who had been commander of the Niagara Light Dragoons in the War of 1812 and builder of the Welland Canal. Henry and Catherine had much in common, for she had spent much of her life working with the United Empire Loyalist Association. Often, reported *Saturday Night* magazine, she wrote and acted in amateur plays showing the Loyalist cause and the hardships suffered by those Britishers whose loyalty to the crown came before personal profit and advantage.

Her favourite nieces, Catherine and Helen, were readily accepted and supported by Pellatt. His own niece, Mary, whom he referred to as "girl" out of apparent respect for his dead wife, was sent on a trip to Europe in 1929. Pellatt also sponsored a "coming out" dance for her eighteenth birthday, as was then the fashion. Unfortunately, the remarriage was brief; the second Mrs. Pellatt died of cancer just before Christmas in 1929.

The Depression forced the sale of Pellatt's 78 Crescent Road home in Rosedale and the Mary Lake estate, which was purchased by the Basilian Order of the Roman Catholic church and today is the Marylake monastery of the Augustinian order. Pellatt moved to 62A Bernard Avenue, a small New Toronto house. Sir Henry was now in his seventies and, ignoring the fact that he had lost considerable weight, continued to wear his enormous and elegantly tailored clothes. He suffered temporary blindness, and his niece Mary and her mother often took turns reading to him, sometimes "days at a time".

Remaining with Pellatt faithfully until the end was Tom Ridgeway, a war veteran, world traveller and chauffeur from the Casa Loma days who became cook, housekeeper, valet and companion to Sir Henry. Pellatt also took a few cherished possessions with him to Bernard Avenue, including a large desk that he claimed had once belonged to Napoleon and some rugs that had to be "folded double" to fit the small rooms.

In 1937, the Kiwanis Club asked Sir Henry to return to Casa Loma as guest speaker at their regular luncheon meeting. This was Pellatt's second and last visit to the castle since 1924. The *Globe* reported that "as he gazed around at the castle about which he had dreamed for so many years, the old man's eyes filled with tears. When he rose to speak, emotion choked his words and Sir Henry covered his face with his hands." A true gentleman to the end, he said, "I built Casa Loma principally as a place where people would enjoy themselves. Your club is now using it for that purpose and bringing enjoyment and happiness to countless people. . . . It could not be put to a better use. I am satisfied."

Pellatt's last hurrah came in January 1939. The Queen's Own Rifles threw an eightieth birthday party for their old commander. It was a reunion of the regiment that Pellatt had taken to England in 1910. Almost one-quarter of the regiment—most white-haired themselves by this time—came to the dinner in Toronto's exclusive Royal York Hotel. A remnant of the 1910 Queen's Own Rifles band played with what was left of their well-worn and battered old instruments. The men paraded to the regimental march and sang:

Sir Henry Pellatt, late in life

The Queen's Own Rifles they came this way,
And broke things up in an awful way,
You can bet your life there'll be hell to pay
When the Queen's Own Rifles come back this way.

Politicians gave speeches. A telegram was read from Queen Mary: "Your Colonel-in-Chief has great pleasure in sending you warmest congratulations on the occasion of your eightieth birthday." Handshakes, cheers, jokes and stories brought back memories of past days. Sir Henry's speech was brief. "I am more than pleased to be well enough to see you all and to wish you godspeed in the future. . . . I am delighted to see all the boys again but," he added with a smile, "you look like men now."

On March 8, 1939, Sir Henry Mill Pellatt died. Three days later, thousands lined downtown Toronto streets to watch the funeral procession. Drums muffled in black beat a low tattoo as they waited in the sombre dullness of the

Funeral service for Sir Henry Pellatt inside the Toronto Armories

late winter dusk. After the funeral in St. James Cathedral, a gun carriage bearing the casket—topped by the white and scarlet feathers of Sir Henry's cocked hat lying upon his sword of ivory and gold—was drawn along King Street. Rifles reversed, the soldiers of the Queen's Own Rifles closed in around the carriage. Sir Henry's decorations, displayed on a purple cushion, were carried by the regimental sergeant-major who followed on foot. The reversed boots of an honoured soldier swung in the stirrups as the riderless stallion pranced behind the gun carriage. While the regimental band played a dirge, the entire procession moved west on King to University Avenue and then north to Richmond Street, where a hearse was waiting to bear the casket to Sir Henry's final resting place. At the mausoleum on Yonge Street, immediately north of what is now Highway 401, the men of the 1910 bugle band blew "Last Post" and "Reveille". Sir Henry Mill Pellatt's life ended the way he had enjoyed it most, full of pomp and ceremony.

Further Reading

Barnard, W.T. *The Queen's Own Rifles of Canada, 1860-1960.* Toronto: Ontario Publishing Co., 1960.

Denison, Merrill. *The People's Power: The History of Ontario Hydro.* Toronto: McClelland and Stewart, 1974.

Griffin, Frederick. *A Gentleman of Toronto: Sir Henry Mill Pellatt.* Toronto, c. 1930.

Kilbourn, William, ed. *The Toronto Book: An Anthology of Writings Past and Present.* Toronto: Macmillan, 1976.

Spigelman, Martin. *Wilfrid Laurier.* Don Mills, Ont.: Fitzhenry & Whiteside, 1978.

Sturgis, James. *Adam Beck.* Don Mills, Ont.: Fitzhenry & Whiteside, 1978.

Pellatt of Toronto

Credits

The publishers wish to express their gratitude to the following who have given permission to use copyrighted illustrations in this book:

City of Toronto Archives (The James Collection), pages 3, 14, 16, 23, 33, 40, 41, 42, 44, 46, 50, 53, 55, 57, 58, 62, 63
Claude Neon Ltd., frontispiece
Metropolitan Toronto Library Board, pages 34, 36, 38
Ontario Archives, pages 7, 8
Ontario Hydro, pages 24, 27, 29
Mary Pellatt, pages 17, 60
Public Archives of Canada, pages 19 (C4706), 21 (C19348), 31 (C16390)
Queens University Archives, page 11

Editor: Cathleen Hoskins

Every effort has been made to credit all sources correctly. The author and publishers will welcome any information that will allow them to correct any errors or omissions.

Index